So You Want to Be Mentored........

But Can You Handle It???

By: Mary Blue

Copyright © 2006 by Mary Blue

So You Want To Be Mentored...
But Can You Handle It???
by Mary Blue

Printed in the United States of America

ISBN 1-60034-294-9

All rights reserved solely by the author. The author guarantees all contents are original and do not infringe upon the legal rights of any other person or work. No part of this book may be reproduced in any form without the permission of the author. The views expressed in this book are not necessarily those of the publisher.

Unless otherwise indicated, all Scripture quotations are from the King James Version of the Bible. Copyright © 1978 The Moody Bible Institute of Chicago. Used by permission

www.xulonpress.com

Table of Contents

Foreword vii
Acknowledgments ix
Introduction xi

The Mentors in My Life 15

Becoming a Naomi 23

Am I Ready for This? 29

Do I Know Who I Am? 33

Do I Need Emotional Healing? 39

Am I Harboring Unforgiveness? 47

Do I Have a Prayer Life? 55

Do I Know My Gifting?..............................61

Can I Take Instruction?..............................67

What Exactly Am I Looking For?...............73

How do I Find a Mentor?...........................79

Foreword

How befitting that God would choose a wife, mother, and intercessor to teach and challenge other women from the topic of Mentorship. Mary Blue has had a mothering heart from her youth. But who would have known the countless numbers of women who have and will be blessed by Mary D. Blue's life in Christ.

She writes and teaches practical yet profound revelations concerning our value and responsibility as sons and daughters in the Kingdom of God.

She has a heart that is committed and surrendered to do the whole will of God. I believe she has been anointed to Call Forth, Nurture, Activate and Release women into their proper positions as spiritual mothers and mentors. She has a special assignment to reveal the precious and priceless treasure of motherhood and to call forth mothers who are so desperately needed in this hour. I pray that this book will be a blessing to the Body of Christ starting in the United States and reaching abroad.

Patrice R. Osiris
Educator, Exhorter, Mentor and Mentee
Minister, Teacher, Speaker

Acknowledgments

I would be remiss if I dare acknowledge anyone before I give glory to God, without whom this would not be possible. I thank God for the guidance He gave as I penned not only the words but even the title of this book.

I'd like to thank my husband who was patient and shared his time as I lived the life of a mentor.

I appreciate my editors: David, my friend and literary obstetrician. He encouraged me as I labored over this work—and was indeed the one who convinced me early on that "the baby was still in there." It was the perfect motivational comment to say to a labor and delivery nurse. Thanks to Dionne, my daughter and friend, who put her academic expertise to work on this project; and did not spare the red pen simply because I was her mother.

Thank you Ms. Ann (Mom) for being my first real example of a mentor.

I can't forget my other children, Leah and Alex, who never cease to encourage me to 'go for it'.

So You Want To Be Mentored...

To all my mentors over the years whether active or silent, natural or spiritual; thank you for pouring into me, loving me and nurturing me as I grew into who you knew I was. Thank you for continuing to be available to me First Lady Jakes, Mother Peterson, Mama Smith, the Bells, Mama Blue—my mother-in-love, and my aunt Laura Bell who along with my high school home economics teacher, Mrs. Tyler, passed on their love for baking. All of my neighbors thank you.

To my many teachers over the years that were able to see beyond the stuttering little girl and encourage me to reach for things I could not see.

I can't forget my girl Verna who allowed me to be her Naomi even when she didn't need it. Verna, you were always **'for me'**. Thank you.

To all who I have mentored, I pray that you will go on to do the same for someone else.

I'd like to thank Kenneth, who lit a fire under me to complete this book just by completing his book first.

Also, to all of those that prayed me through the rough places in my life and allowed me to be human, many thanks.

Lastly, I thank each of you that have believed in me and in the mentoring process by purchasing this book. I pray that what is written within these pages will strengthen and challenge you to reach out as a mentor, or to grow as you receive from the mentors God has placed in your life.

Mary Blue

Introduction

"And Ruth said, Entreat me not to leave thee, or to return from following after thee: for whither thou goest, I will go; and where thou lodgest, I will lodge: thy people shall be my people, and thy God my God: Where thou diest, will I die, and there will I be buried: the Lord do so to me, and more also, if aught but death part thee and me."
(Ruth 1:16-17; KJV)

In the book of Ruth, Ruth marries Naomi's son. She'd undoubtedly developed a mother-daughter relationship with Naomi. Her loyalty to Naomi indicates this.

Once Naomi's husband and sons died, Ruth and her sister-in-law had the option to go back to the house of their fathers. Her sister-in-law chose to do just that. Naomi even encouraged them to do so. Ruth refused.

I believe it was solely out of relationship with Naomi. She clung to Naomi and told her that only death could separate them. I know of no other statement that could imply such a strong bond between two individuals.

In my early years, I didn't set out to become a mentor. In fact, I myself was a Ruth in need of a Naomi. When I became a Christian in 1975 at the age of twenty-one I was completely unfamiliar with the Bible story of Ruth.

The beauty of Ruth and Naomi's relationship is that later in the short book of Ruth we see the mentoring aspect of the relationship develop more clearly. Naomi was very instrumental in instructing Ruth on how to conduct herself in the presence of Boaz, her perspective kinsman redeemer/husband.

Because of her background, Naomi was familiar with the laws of Israel whereas Ruth was not. Naomi became the individual that could take Ruth to places in her life and development where she had previously not been, which is the nature of a mentoring relationship.

The Webster's Dictionary definition of a mentor is one who serves as a trusted counselor or teacher to another person. In laymen's terms it is simply someone who is spiritually and naturally mature, who has walked through the obstacles of life and has survived to tell the tale.

The one who becomes your mentor may have battle scars but the key is they survived! And they are willing to share the story of their journey with you.

In my mentoring relationships (the Naomis that God brought into my life) I initially didn't recognize that I was being mentored, nor did I recognize God's hand in placing those women in my life. Even though each of those women significantly impacted me, to me they were just my moms.

I share my personal experience and what I have learned in the hopes that you will be able to acknowledge and glean from those God has called to mentor you and that you will be able to reach out and effectively mentor the Ruths that He places in your life.

Although this book is written from a female point of view, its principles are by no means limited to just women. I dare say that men seeking mentors must do so by way of the same road.

Consequently, while I write as a woman and use examples in the lives of women, this is not race nor gender specific but a tool by which anyone can navigate their approach toward a healthy mentoring experience.

Although my mentors have all been women, this does not mean you can not be mentored by the opposite sex. However, because mentoring is a very personal and intimate relationship, be careful that you do not blur or cross the lines, emotionally or physically. You want to ensure that you maintain a healthy mentoring relationship and nothing more.

The Mentors in My Life

My First Naomi

Even without understanding the role of a mentor, it was natural for me to observe women that had been Christians longer than I had or who had just lived longer. God blessed my life with such a woman who I began to call Mom.

Mrs. Richardson was a woman of prayer and wisdom. I was not a believer yet. Her son introduced us as he and I went to college together. However, very soon we had a separate relationship that did not include her son.

The relationship between she and I developed naturally. We just hit it off without much effort. She was such a great listener that I began to visit her during my down time or between classes.

If I was frustrated, disheartened or just needing to talk, no matter what I was going through this woman was always available for me. Her soft-spoken wisdom always included the Lord.

At the time, I didn't know I was being mentored—I only knew that I was being loved and nurtured.

You have to understand that up to that point I only related mentoring to the Boys and Girls Club or the Big Brother and Big Sister programs that were geared toward academics and socialization. This Ruth and Naomi relationship was foreign to me.

Until her death in 1993, Mrs. Richardson was always a sounding board and a safe haven for me. Long after college and even across the miles I could always count on her listening ear and understanding heart.

Mama Richardson deposited many nuggets of truth in my spirit during my formative years as a young Christian from 1975-1985:
- During that time I learned that prayer would always lead me from a dark place to one of light;
- She taught me to trust God even if I could not trace His hand or understand His plan because He was faithful; and
- She also taught me that things were not always as bad after a good night's sleep.

A Career Mentor

I attended Rutgers University College of Nursing. During the time that I attended there were very few role models for people of color. In fact there was only one black professor in the entire college. Her name was Bobby.

Bobby took it upon herself to keep me abreast of opportunities that became available that I would have otherwise not known about. Because of her I received an application for Who's Who in Colleges and Universities and was accountable to her to get it in by the deadline.

Prior to meeting Bobby, I had never heard of Who's Who.

I had the good fortune to be selected by Who's Who and to blaze a trail of academic success for my children to follow.

Bobby also checked on my grades and whatever else she had to do to ensure my success. If I wanted to graduate, she was going to ensure that I did what I said I would do.

A Second Mother

During those formative years there was another precious Naomi that showed up like an angel of mercy in a time of need.

I'd just delivered our youngest daughter and my own mother was unable to be with me. Mrs. Smith worked in the newborn nursery. As I was attempting to nurse my daughter and struggling to do so, she stepped in to help me.

I will never forget the day that Mrs. Smith reached out to me. She didn't do it as a nurse, but as a mother helping her daughter through something that she had already walked through. We bonded that day as Naomi and Ruth.

We have maintained our relationship over the decades, keeping in touch by phone two to three times a year. As a matter of fact one of my favorite Christmas recipes is 'apple cake'; every time I make it I think of her: a tangible reminder of her life and influence.

Mrs. Smith was a mentor I would go to for advice on handling people, especially at work. She was a master at dealing with people. I learned a lot by watching and listening to her interactions with others.

I share this because mentors can serve different purposes in your life if you are open to it. To this day, Mrs. Smith remains one of my most precious treasures.

What My Mother Taught Me

Along with these two women that God placed in my life as mentors was my own mother. Mothers are in a position to be natural mentors.

Even though I didn't grow up in a Christian home, my mother taught me the difference between right and wrong.

She also taught me the meaning of "*a friend in need is a friend indeed*." As a child, I remember hearing my mom repeat that little rhyme; although I didn't fully understand it until I was an adult.

Through the years I watched my mom exhibit loyalty when things were tough for her friends and everyone else bailed. She always remained firm to help her friends through their crises'.

My mother displayed through her actions that you shouldn't call yourself a friend if no one can count on you to be there during the difficult times.

I learned from this to distinguish the associates in my life from those who were true friends. There is a distinct difference between the two. An associate is a casual acquaintance but a friend loves at all times.

My mother also taught me that I *am* my brother's keeper. My two older siblings and I all experienced the teen years together. My mom would allow us to go out as long as we stayed together and looked out for each other. Under no circumstances were we to split up and go our separate ways. We had to be accountable to and for one another.

Mentored By A Couple

I graduated from college three years later than my peers. To finish school, I often went part-time while I worked. Although it was more difficult than being a full-time student, I'd gained a real sense of stick-to-it-ness from my moms (along with their lavish love and encouragement).

After graduation, I joined the Army Nurse Corps. Soon after entering the Corps, I met my future husband and we were married two months later.

No, I was not pregnant, just in case you are wondering. I agreed to marry him after much thought and prayer.

In 1990 my family moved to Chesterfield, Virginia, where my husband and I attended a Sunday school class called "Young Marrieds". Bill and Barbara Bell who had been married thirty years taught the class.

By this time we'd been married for ten years and were one of the older couples in the class in age and years of marriage.

This was my first experience being mentored by a couple, which I enjoyed very much. The Bells helped to strengthen me during some very difficult times.

Remember I said my husband and I were married only two months after meeting. Despite the fact that God said "yes," marriage so soon after meeting has a set of unique challenges.

Even though we were married, we didn't really know each other; a process that developed over time.

As a couple, our relationship with the Bells gave us somewhere to go to be vulnerable and to vent. It was also the first time I realized that there was a difference in what people perceive about your marriage and what really *is* your marriage.

It released me from looking at others and comparing my husband or my marriage to theirs'. Hearing about the Bells' marital struggles gave me hope that things do get better.

Barbara played two roles for me: a big sister as well as a mom. Bill was like a father to me, always available to comfort me with gentle guidance and prayer. Because they were also more than fifteen years our senior, their experiences in life were extremely helpful.

One evening I felt I had tried all I could try to talk to my husband. I was weary of the effort and frustrated with the feeling of swimming upstream. I felt I had two choices: I could leave or I could call Bill. I called Bill and said, "I need my Dad!"

Bill's response was, "You got him!" He listened until I was empty. He then counseled me and prayed for me until I was peaceful and revived enough to go on. This is only one of the many instances of Bill or Barbara being available to me.

Becoming a Naomi

The Big Transition

It was during the season in my life when the Bells were mentoring me that I made the transition from being solely a Ruth to becoming a Naomi. I was beginning to be called upon by the younger women of the church for counsel.

Although I didn't feel I was qualified to handle their questions and issues, Barbara encouraged me by constantly commenting on my level of wisdom.

In fact, Barbara often talked to me with pen and paper in hand to write down what she considered the nuggets that I would share. Although I disagreed with her assessment of my level of maturity and wisdom, her encouragement gave me the courage to step out and share.

While I was dealing with my own issues I found myself pouring into the lives of others. I discovered that God doesn't always wait until you feel you are in a good position to pour out to someone else. However, He does make sure to have a filling station available. In other words he provides someone to pour into you so that you are not empty. The Bells were that filling station for me.

I have a friend who shares my birthday, though she is eleven years my junior. At the time, she was the mother of three with a fourth on the way.

I didn't realize it until much later, by way of a letter she wrote to me, that in our interactions I'd begun to teach her from my own experience.

Whether it was cooking, cleaning, parenting or being a wife, we developed a Naomi-Ruth relationship that grew out of our friendship.

Throughout our relationship, whatever was going on, we always found our way to the Word of God and His counsel through prayer.

To date, my friend and her husband have successfully raised five wonderful children and she has indeed become a woman of prayer. And I know that like me she has gone on to become a mentor.

I like to think of her as a mentor born from the birth canal of our mentoring relationship. I believe more mentors are birthed this way than simply by circumstantial need.

The difference between the two is that birthing a mentor happens when you mentor well. The mentored one goes on to become like-minded.

Circumstantial need would be an ill prepared Ruth stepping up to the plate to help a young woman coming up behind her because no one else is available.

Grow Up, Your Ruth Is Waiting!

There are times when there seem to be a shortage of Naomis. This could be from a lack of experienced godly women, or because the potential Naomi doesn't recognize or can't accept her season to be a Ruth is over.

Sometimes a woman doesn't recognize the need to grow up in the things of God. I often run across women who have a real problem with aging. They find it difficult to reconcile what they see in the mirror with what they think or how they feel. They are emotional Peter Pans, forever refusing to grow up.

I have an aunt who told me she was thirty-nine years old so many times when I was younger that she actually forgot how old she was.

Women who refuse to grow up can push the younger women away and discourage them by their lack of time, attention and constructive input. I believe this leads to a generation that not only has not been mentored but who don't know how to mentor those coming after them.

The Bible instructs those of us that are older to teach the younger women. I believe the same has to be true for men. Older more mature men must teach the younger men.

For example, Elisha was mentored by Elijah the prophet. Elisha, who didn't know he was a prophet at the time, went on to become one of the greatest prophets in the Bible.

Give What you Have

Even if you are seeking a mentor of your own, it does not let you off the hook of being a mentor for someone else.

Not everyone is cut out to be a mentor. Mentoring is an unselfish act of kindness even though it can be inconvenient.

Personally, I believe that all relationships are inconvenient; so unless you are a hermit, loving someone else will eventually inconvenience you.

Whatever the situation, if you are reading this book and you have been married a while, have parented or have lived longer than thirty years, then you can mentor someone who has not.

I'm not implying that you don't need a mentor yourself. I'm simply trying to clarify that you can give what you've already received. This also applies to singles mentoring other singles—personally or professionally—therefore; you are not off the hook.

You don't have to wait until you have a mentor to share knowledge and wisdom with someone who is not as far along the road as you are in age or maturity.

Granted it does require maturity, but I learned from a pastor friend of mine that God only gives to us so we can give it again.

If you have nuggets of wisdom, share them. There is no race that he who dies with the most nuggets wins. Give what you can while you seek what you need.

Am I Ready for This?

"Examine me, O Lord, and prove me; try my reins and my heart.."
(Psalm 26:2: KJV)

You may wonder why I chose to deal with this topic first, before telling you how to find a mentor.

I've met a lot of women over the years that talk of mentorship and seem to have a longing to have **someone** show them 'the way'.

However, after being a mentor, I've found that it is imperative to do a self-evaluation before you seek a mentor (I speak from the position of a Naomi).

Sometimes people have issues that no amount of mentoring will fix. No matter how many phone calls you make to the mentor or how you phrase 'it' today

(**It** is the drama at hand—the situation or problem the mentee is calling about).

For example, if you are dealing with the negative effects of molestation in a relationship, perhaps you need to seek counseling.

The role of a mentor is not to fix anything. If something is broken in your life, it is only Jesus, the Master Builder who is able to mend it. He is the repairer of the breach, no mater how the breach occurred.

Nor is it a mentor's job to try to piece together in short order what has taken years to pull apart.

People sometimes approach the mentoring relationship as they would a doctor's visit. They go in with a laundry list of symptoms and expect the mentor to diagnose their condition and give them the right prescription. That job belongs to the Great Physician and should not be expected from the mentor.

The first step for you in looking for a mentor is to stand before a spiritual mirror and decide whether you are ready to be mentored; whether you can take it.

By definition, a mentor is someone, usually older and more experienced who provides advice and support to, and watches over and fosters the progress of, a younger, less experienced person.

You might wonder, "Why would I be afraid of that? It sounds exactly like what I'm looking for."

Being mentored means being confronted on issues that you have heretofore ignored. It means being accountable to another person and giving them permission to bring correction to your life if necessary. This can be a very uncomfortable situation.

In addition, being that transparent can cause you to feel very vulnerable.

If what I just said frightens you, keep looking in the mirror: you may not be quite ready for mentoring. Not every season in your life is ripe for mentoring.

Below are some important questions you need to consider before you search out or evaluate someone to consider for a mentor:

1. Do I know who I am?
2. Do I need emotional healing?
3. Am I harboring unforgiveness in my heart?
4. Do I have a prayer life?
5. Do I know my gifting?
6. Can I take instruction?

At this stage in your life you may not agree that these issues are important or relevant. However, from a mentor's point of view, knowing the answers to these questions will determine your success or failure in the mentoring relationship.

Let's look at these questions one at a time.

Do I Know Who I Am?

"Search me, O God, and know my heart: try me, and know my thoughts: And see if there be any wicked way in me, And lead me in the way everlasting."
                    (Psalm 139: 23, 24; KJV)

During my first mentoring experience I did not yet understand who I was, especially in my relationship with the Lord. Even though those were the days of *finding yourself*, I didn't have much of a clue as to why I existed.

The only thing I solidly knew was that I loved serving, so I started there and later added a growing experience and understanding of prayer.

Faithful as He is, the Lord began to show me my heart. Things I thought were natural to being human, I discovered were God-given specifically to me. I began to understand that my tenderness of heart, my affinity to turn everything into a teaching moment and my growing love for prayer were all windows to help me to see myself more clearly.

One of the issues I dealt with before I met Jesus was low self-esteem. After I became a Christian, I sought to understand who I was in Christ by reading aloud scriptures of affirmation to myself.

If you do not yet understand that you are the righteousness of God in Christ Jesus or that you are more than a conqueror, you don't need a mentor; you need more personal time in the Word in Bible study.

If that is the case, this is not an indictment against you. To be successfully mentored you must know who you are in Christ. This is a foundation for a good mentoring experience. It's not impossible to be mentored if you don't know who you are in Christ; but it can be a lot more difficult for your mentor. However if you are willing, this is something that can be learned from a mentor.

What Does He Say About Me?

There is such a thing as self-talk. Paul counsels us in Ephesians 5:19a to speak to ourselves in psalms, hymns and spiritual songs. In I Samuel 30:6b David encouraged himself in the Lord his God. Self-talk is speaking a truth about you to you.

If I were to ask you to your face "who are you?" would you give me your name or occupation? Just as I had to, you must discern the difference between who you are and what you do.

I am a nurse by profession, but regardless of my profession, I would still be the righteousness of God in Christ Jesus.

You see, who you are can only truly be discovered when you connect with the One who made you. Only then can you understand the blueprint of your life and the purpose for which you were created.

I believe I was born to be a nurse, but my nursing would be no more than academic prowess without Christ.

My position as a child of God enables me to nurture my patients, to pray for them and minister to them out of Christ's love.

I've seen nurses that were academically brilliant—that could pass a Nasogastric tube down your nose quicker than Superman could fly—however their impact on their patients stopped there. They were conducting learned tasks. They were good at the skill but the heart didn't line up with the head.

If Jesus lives in your heart, you can do what you do much better than someone that may appear academically more superior or more qualified than you.

If you need help in this area, get one of those little promise books. Read it. Recognize the promises of God in your life and begin to speak them out loud to yourself.

I Peter 5:17 tells us that faith comes by hearing the Word of God. Once your faith is built up, you can begin to have the confidence to walk in who God says you are.

Dreamer or Visionary?

If you were paying attention you were just given a key to open the door to self-discovery. Your first assignment is to focus on what God says, not what men say about you. If I'd allowed others to define who I am, I shudder to think of where I'd be or what I'd be doing.

There will be times when nobody believes in you, but you! Don't let the small minds of others dictate your future. Don't be put in a box by the expectations of others.

Look at Joseph. His brothers called him a dreamer when he was actually a man with a vision who dared to believe God.

When you are the only one who believes your dreams, dream anyway. There are no guarantees that you'll be understood. But the reality is that being understood is not a prerequisite to greatness.

In fact, I can think of many great people who were sorely misunderstood. Job was misunderstood by his own wife, who urged him to curse God and die. Job's friends were convinced of his sin and his prideful unwillingness to admit it.

John was misunderstood even from conception. John's father struggled in believing God concerning his son's birth.

Lastly, let's look at Jesus. He knew exactly who He was and what He had to do. He didn't need the approval of the people to stay focused on the fact that He was the Son of God and that He came to give His life as a ransom for many, including you and me.

During His ministry Jesus always kept His eye focused on the Father and the Father's will. That's how focused you must be on who God says you are.

Your vision might be in its infancy. You may only understand in part what God is doing in and through you, but choose to nurture the part you know like you would a baby.

Give yourself personal time as well as time with God in order to fully develop and come to a place of maturity.

If you want to know what anyone thinks of you let it be Jesus. His opinion is the one that really matters for your destiny.

Once you have a firm handle on who you are, then you are ready to move on to the next step: looking inside your heart.

Contemplation Time

1. What have I heard other people say about me?

_____
_____
_____

2. What is true and what is just talk?

_____
_____
_____

3. Who do I think I am?

_____
_____
_____

4. Who does God say I am?

_____
_____
_____

Do I Need Emotional Healing?

"To appoint unto them that mourn in Zion, to give unto them beauty for ashes, the oil of joy for mourning, the garment of praise for the spirit of heaviness, that they might be called trees of righteousness, the planting of the Lord, that he might be glorified."
(Isaiah 61:3; KJV)

During the summer of 1988 I was on a personal emotional rollercoaster. I'd been married for seven years and it had been mostly rocky. My husband and I had a lot of communication issues.

Added to our communication problems were our frequent moves from state to state with the military, which made it difficult to establish relationships with sound role models.

During that season in my life, God became my wonderful counselor and began to be my help. He gave me instruction on being a wife and correction when I needed it. All of this was done by way of my increasing relationship with the Lord through prayer.

Even though God was mending what was broken in our marriage, I still had incurred emotional damage and dashed expectations during our routine knock down, drag out arguments.

My girlfriend Valerie invited me to go to a Joyce Meyer meeting. Previously, I had only heard her on the radio but was anxious for the opportunity to see her live. Attending that meeting showed me how much I needed help.

Joyce did a visual presentation of Romans the 12th chapter. That particular chapter speaks of every part of the body having a different but important function. Her presentation consisted of placing a ring on her left eye, which was complaining that it never got to wear nice jewelry.

Once the ring was in position, she held her head back in order to hold it in place, thereby hindering the eye from seeing-which was its natural function.

Surprisingly, God used that to let me know that I couldn't take my rightful place in the body if I didn't know what that was. Also, as she began to be transparent about some of her own emotional trauma, I realized there was life after trauma.

A friend at church told me about a book by Linda Dillow called <u>Healing for Damaged Emotions</u>. God used that as a tool to bring restoration to my life and healing to my damaged emotions.

The book had a separate workbook that asked pointed questions about the results of emotional damage on an individual.

I could have chosen to ignore these and not answer the questions. However, I was desperate for healing and felt my honest answers were a life raft for my marriage and my peace of mind.

In addition, I started getting up at 5 a.m. to pray for my family as well as myself (something I wasn't used to doing). I prayed the Word of God since I knew God always honors His Word. I couldn't change my husband but I could work on me.

My getting up ahead of my family to pray was part of a God given strategy to further increase my emotional healing.

One of the scriptures I spoke over myself was Proverbs 31:26: "*She openeth her mouth with wisdom; and in her tongue is the law of kindness.*"

A symptom of me needing healing was yelling at my children. Hence I used scriptures like medicine to deal directly with the symptoms.

As I began to heal I learned to apply scripture in this way even when praying for my children. For example, my younger daughter was a real tattletale. I began to pray Proverbs 11:13 over her.

That scripture states: "*a talebearer revealeth secrets: but he that is of a faithful spirit concealeth the matter.*" I prayed that she would not be a talebearer but that she would be of a faithful spirit.

Today this daughter is one of the most faithful, trustworthy people that I have the pleasure of knowing. She is a loyal friend and a secret keeper. I share this to remind you that the Word does work!

Don't Settle For Salve!

There are certain issues we must settle with God and not with a mentor. Personally, I had to make the effort to get the healing I needed even though I knew I had someone I could call if I was having an especially down day.

I heard Dr. Claudette Copeland say once that "even though God does **the** work, we have to do **some** work." As I said before, we cannot expect a mentor to have the wherewithal to mend what God alone can mend.

Women have a tendency to seek salve for their wounds, not debridement and subsequent healing. Salve is something you use for an immediate soothing, like liniment. It doesn't change the degree of injury; it only gets you through the night.

Some people use alcohol, others might use sex, food or romance novels; anything that will take away the pain for a moment, a quick fix.

I know about quick fixes. Mine was romance novels. I could be transported instantly into a fantasy land where the couples always talked and worked things out without fighting.—I would hide in these novels.

Meanwhile, my own relationship was still broken. I left my own fields untended and wasted valuable time in fantasy land.

No matter what escape mechanism you use, when you come back to earth, you still have to deal with the pain in your own heart.

Instead of using salve on a situation that needs healing, allow the Lord to debride it. Debridement is the scrubbing away of old infected tissue in order to expose the wound underneath so it can be treated and begin healing.

Understand that this is not a comfortable process. In fact, having worked in orthopedic medicine, I've seen the discomfort of patients after the procedure. It sometimes looks as though it will never heal. It bleeds and looks raw, but once the wound is exposed, it can be properly dressed and treated. Soon you will begin to see the tissue granulation that indicates healing.

Though healing was already in progress, it took time before it became evident for all to see. This is important to note because you don't want your mentoring experience to be like a salve that makes you feel better for the moment but doesn't get to the real issues.

Face The Pain

In addition, if you seek to be mentored before you seek healing, your wounds may not heal properly because the scabs may be repeatedly knocked off. A mentor may unwittingly cause you to bleed, which will eventually do more harm than good.

For example, if correction without softness takes you back to memories of being a child standing before your mom as she belittled you, counseling may be needed before mentoring.

Some people don't want to be emotionally healed. They use their pain like a pair of well-used crutches. They park in the handicapped spaces of life and use it to get attention or manipulate the lives of others.

I know this sounds harsh but I've seen it time and time again. If you've gone through several mentors or even can't seem to find a church home that suits you; it may be time to start looking at yourself and not other people.

It's certainly easier and definitely less painful to point the finger at someone else. But the objective here is wholeness. Ignoring your own pain or dysfunction doesn't make it go away. I've found that no matter how far away I tried to go, like a loyal pet, my pain was always waiting for me when I got home.

So you see, you're not the ***only one*** going through this. Of course, that is what the enemy wants you to think to keep you away from wholeness. He knows you're handicapped as long as you hide it or hide from it.

Galatians 5:1 states "*Stand fast, therefore in the liberty where with Christ hath made us free, and be not entangled again with the yoke of bondage*" (KJV). You are less able to stand in liberty if you have not allowed God to break your chains in this area.

Begin to see yourself whole and free. Not that you'll never get hurt again by family, friends or church, but once you are healed you learn how to take the scrapes of life to the Lord much faster and easier so they don't fester and become infected.

Contemplation Time

1. Have I examined myself for signs of infection? If not, ask the Lord to point out those hidden places. What are they?

_____
_____
_____

2. How can I give the infected place wholly to the Lord or do I want to nurse it and rehearse it? Write a short note of release to God.

_____
_____
_____

3. How have I parked in a handicapped space of life?

_____
_____
_____

4. What have I done to face my own dysfunctions or am I still playing the blame game?

_____
_____
_____

Am I Harboring Unforgiveness?

"Therefore if thou bring thy gift to the altar, and there rememberest that thy brother hath ought against thee; Leave there thy gift before the altar, go thy way; first be reconciled to thy brother, and then come and offer thy gift."
(Matthew 5:23, 24; KJV)

You deceive yourself if you think you can successfully grow in a mentoring relationship, or be used of God in ministry, without first leaving your gift at the altar and dealing with your issues of offence or unforgiveness.

The Word of God is very clear about forgiveness and its affect on one's relationship with the Father. Matthew 6:14 says, *"For if ye forgive men their trespasses, your heavenly Father will also forgive you"* (KJV). Matthew is clear that we must stand before

Him without harboring unforgiveness toward anyone if we expect Him to forgive us our trespasses.

I've known many people who hold on to a grudge like it was a precious hidden treasure. They regularly check on their grudge to ensure it's still in good condition. Occasionally they show it off to people, beaming with pride over what they hold.

I've known pastors who have taught forgiveness but not walked in it. Before you gasp, remember that clergy are no different from the rest of us humans. They hold a different position in the Body of Christ but they are not exempt from human error.

Relational Isolation

Lack of forgiveness will eat away at the fibers of a relationship like water erodes a coastline.

I've experienced it in my own family among relatives. Sometimes years go by and the one who has offended another goes on with his or her life and may not even be aware of the offense. Whereas the offended one who refuses to forgive walks around shackled by it like a ball and chain.

In the summer of 2005 I was diagnosed with cancer. It was a frightening time in my life, not knowing if the cancer was isolated or if it had metastasized to some other area of my body. I had to have radiation treatments.

Immediately following treatments I became radioactive and had to avoid direct contact with anyone for seven days. That time of isolation seemed extremely long to me and I had to work at keeping myself encouraged.

I share this experience because unforgiveness can be like that cancer. If it is not met with immediate forgiveness it can cause isolation from those you love and those who love you.

Due to my experience with cancer, I have a new understanding of the scripture that reminds us that life is like a vapor. We don't have time to waste on bitterness or unforgiveness.

We can't be about our Father's business if we're shackled by the cancer of unforgiveness. Life is too short to miss opportunities to laugh and to love and generally enjoy its benefits.

Sometimes you can spot a person a mile away that is harboring unforgiveness–they are miserable and unhappy.

It has the opposite effect than what's expected. Instead of punishing someone else by not speaking to them or not interacting with them, we end up punishing ourselves.

The Root of Pride

I realize that at the root of unforgiveness is ***pride.*** It is pride that won't allow us to admit that we are wrong, or allow us to go to someone and sincerely apologize or ask for forgiveness or even to talk a situation out.

The person that offended you may have already apologized to you or asked for forgiveness. But you refused to give it in return. Why? Do you want to punish them for what they did to you?

Now, please don't use this as a tool for serious issues like adultery that require more than just a simple 'I'm sorry'. There are some issues that require counseling because a trust has been broken. I'm referring to things that you've been mad about so long that you have to think really hard to even remember what the original offense was.

People that won't forgive are very difficult to be around because they become obsessed with the offense in order to gain support from others. They become like a politician lobbying for everyone to agree with how they feel about the issue.

These are the kind of people that exhaust you as you interact with them. I call them high maintenance relationships. You spend so much energy dealing with their offense and trying to help them to shake it, that by the time you're done you've had all the energy sucked right out of you.

These are the kind of people that are only happy when they've made everyone around them as miserable as they are and like the radiation, their negativity can spread to whatever it touches.

The Cancer of Unforgiveness

Unforgiveness can operate like a cancer in your spirit and will therefore hinder your ability to be mentored. Your ear will not be open to the instruction of man if you have not heard and obeyed the instruction of the Lord.

A perfect example of this behavior is in the person of King Saul. According to I Samuel chapter 15, he had explicit instructions from God on how to deal with the Amalekites. Samuel told him in detail what God wanted of him. Saul disobeyed the Word of the Lord which led to the kingdom being taken from him and given to David.

Later Saul's bitterness toward the young "would be" King David caused his ultimate demise. Make no mistake about it, bitterness and unforgiveness will eventually destroy anyone foolish enough to allow either to take up residence in their hearts.

If you desire to be used of God or grow in ministry, forgiving others is not an option. You absolutely must forgive those that offend you. The plumb line with which we measure our lives must be Christ.

Like A Little Child

Of course there will be constant opportunities to take offense. But remember, you always have a choice to be offended or not. It requires maturity on the one hand and child-likeness on the other; maturity, because you must recognize the need to continually forgive and child-likeness because it will allow you to respond with the innocence of a child.

When you were a young child you might have gotten upset with one of your playmates but would soon forget about the offense and go back to playing with the very kid that upset you.

The parents of the child would still be steaming over what someone else's child did to their child. Meanwhile, the kids are the best of friends.

Unforgiveness, whether among spouses, siblings, co-workers or any other relationship will doom that relationship to ultimate failure. You must choose to forgive despite what your emotions tell you.

Usually our emotions don't agree with our decision to forgive. Forgive anyway. Your emotions will eventually line up with your decision. Don't allow pride to steer you down a dead end street.

If you are offended by someone and don't forgive them, you allow them power over your life that should not be theirs to hold. **Take your life back**. Make a decision to forgive so that you can fully live.

Also, keep in mind that forgiveness may not be a one time thing. You may even need to forgive the same person multiple times about different offenses. Some relationships require more patience than others.

I want to share this poem that I wrote called 'Regrets and Dreads'.

> *"He's dead to me; she's dead to me; that's what I hear you say.*
>
> *But they're not really dead; they're just not doing things your way.*
>
> *What will you do when you find, they really are dead? You live the rest of your life with regrets and dreads.*
> *So what do I do, you want to know.*
>
> *Forgive. Love on. Cause at the end of life, that's all that will show."*

Contemplation Time

1. What have I learned about harboring unforgiveness?

_____
_____
_____

2. How has unforgiveness handicapped me presently or in the past?

_____
_____
_____

3. Who has power over me because of a grudge that I hold? Why am I holding a grudge?

_____
_____
_____

5. What do I do to ensure I don't harbor unforgiveness or offense?

_____
_____
_____

6. Who do I need to ask for forgiveness?

_____
_____
_____

Do I Have A Prayer Life?

"And he spake a parable unto them to this end, that men ought always to pray and not to faint".
(Luke 18:1; KJV)

I believe I can safely state that you will never see the Lord mightily using anyone on a consistent basis that has not learned the value of prayer. Prayer is always the stepladder to that next level in any area of life that you are seeking.

It is through prayer that the layers of your past are stripped away. It is also through prayer that those broken places are mended. Prayer allows us not only to share with our heavenly Father all of our cares and concerns but it is also the conduit by which He gives us direction and instruction.

In the Bible we see many times where prayer and praise catapulted someone into their destiny. The biblical tribe of Judah was the praise and worship team of Israel. When Israel was preparing to take the Promised Land, Judah went before the people: praise preceded the promise!

In the story of Joseph, it was his brother Judah who suggested the brothers sell Joseph instead of killing him. It was in the plan of God that Joseph go ahead of Israel into Egypt to ensure their future prosperity. Judah, which means praise, propelled him there.

The team of prayer and praise can transition you from a person walking in mediocrity to someone moving in spiritual greatness. And, to get to that great place, and be properly mentored along the way, you must be able to commit problems and concerns to the Lord in prayer.

Prayer First

People often make the mistake of running to the phone to call their mentor every time something goes wrong or when there is a decision to be made. Now mind you, seeking additional prayer or wisdom is perfectly acceptable. But if you begin to think of your mentor before you consider prayer, you have stepped over the line of balance.

No mentor, no matter how wise or anointed, should take the place of the guidance of the Holy Spirit gained through prayer.

I was mentoring a young woman who would sometimes call me three to five times a day for one thing or another. Like the mother I am, I would give her my time and attention and see to her needs.

One day as I was in prayer, the Lord pointed out a mentoring mistake I had made that broke my heart. The young woman had put me in the place of the Holy Spirit and I had allowed it.

She could not see God because I was hindering her and thereby handicapping her. In other words, there was no need for her to pray for guidance when she could take the shortcut and just call me.

I know I'm not the only one who has made that mistake. It is a common mentoring faux pas.

If you need a better picture, consider a mother carrying her child everywhere and never placing the child on the floor. The child's leg muscles don't get a chance to develop properly, as there's no need for that if you're being carried.

The mother thinks she's helping by getting the child where he needs to be in an efficient manner. She wants to keep the child from getting dirty or from falling.

But, if the child is to ever walk independently he must be allowed to stand on his own. He may falter, stumble and yes, even fall; but he will eventually gain the necessary strength needed to stand and finally walk on his own.

Once I realized my error I corrected my mistake by limiting the calls that I would take from the young woman and letting her know I would pray with her, not go get the answer for her.

Patience, Practice And Perseverance

When I was teaching my children to cook I would sometimes get impatient with the slowness of their progress and complete the task myself. If you are a parent you may have encountered a similar situation. But if you are the mentor, be lovingly patient. Progress may be slower than you'd like but someone had to wait for you.

If you are the mentored, stay the course. My daughter is over thirty years old and still calls to ask how to make certain foods. Everything gets easier with practice and perseverance. Continue to seek the Lord in prayer yourself.

A mentor is merely directing you on the runway of life. His or her words should be no more than confirmation of what you've already gleaned from the Holy Spirit in prayer. In addition, the Holy Spirit cannot navigate you to the appointed destination if prayer is not your compass.

Imagine being on a ship in the middle of the ocean with no land in sight. Without navigational equipment you won't know which direction to go.

If you don't care where you land, then prayer isn't necessary. However, if you don't want to waste time or walk in undue stress, use prayer as your guide to get to your proper destination.

So You Want To Be Mentored...

Contemplation Time

1. Do I have a special time in the day that belongs only to God? How do I use that time?

_____
_____
_____
_____

2. What is the first thing I do when there is trouble?

_____
_____
_____
_____
_____

3. How is prayer important to me?

_____
_____
_____
_____

4. Do I need to make a commitment to begin spending time with God? (Even if it's five minutes a day, it's a start.)

_____
_____
_____
_____

Do I Know My Gifting?

"Now concerning spiritual gifts, brethren, I would not have you ignorant."
(I Corinthians 12:1; KJV)

If you are wondering why this is a necessary question, consider for a minute being a carpenter's apprentice when your actual goal is to become a plumber. You must find a mentor commiserate with your gifting.

If you have the gift of healing, do you want someone who only operates in the interpretation of tongues? Likewise, if you are an intercessor, your mentor should know something of prayer and meditation. A gifted administrator cannot be your example if your goal is to become an orator.

If you consider the matter in prayer, the Holy Spirit will guide you to the proper mentor in order to guide your steps to the proper place. However, it is helpful if you first seek out your own gift and purpose. Understanding this will be part of knowing where you are headed and what you bring to the Kingdom table.

It is <u>not necessarily</u> the role of the mentor to determine your gifting for you, though it is not uncommon for her/him to point out what they observe in your life.

Every Gift Has Its Place

I remember some years ago when I was whining to God about not having a gift. My husband was a beautiful singer and all I did was serve people, take meals to the sick and shut-in and pray.

I was under the false impression that if you were gifted you could sing like Mahalia or Aretha, or preach like Bishop T. D. Jakes. I had no idea how many gifts were required to make the body of Christ function properly.

The Lord took me to I Corinthians, chapter 12 and began to instruct me through prayer and listening to the Holy Spirit. I didn't know anything about the ministry of helps or the diversity of the gifts God had given to His children. I only knew what I saw and heard from others.

But according to the Word of God, if we were all fingers where would the eyes be? If we were all eyes, where would the legs be? After a thorough reading of I Corinthians 12, I realized that I had to get rid of the notion of one gift being more important than another.

It is a common misconception in the body of Christ that some gifts are more important than others. Even if we don't say it, our actions tend to ascribe more weight to some than to others.

I really did think that everyone was called to be a servant and a helper. I was wrong. God placed something in each of us that is ours alone. As I matured, He added to me but always for His glory and in His timing.

To Everything There is a Season

In due time, God will bring out of you what He has placed in you. Due time is not on your clock; it is only on God's timetable. David is a wonderful example for us. He knew when he was still a Shepherd that he was really a king just waiting for his season.

Let me take a moment here to encourage you to recognize the seasons of your life (Read Ecclesiastes 3:1). If David had left his shepherding as soon as he knew he was anointed king, he wouldn't have been able to slay Goliath. Why not?

It was in caring for his flock that he obtained the skill and experience to be a *giant* killer. It was when he was all alone in the fields that he learned the true meaning of worship. It was in keeping his father's sheep that he learned responsibility over what he was given. These are the elements God used to make him a great king unlike his predecessor Saul.

We may think we are ready for something when we are not. If you are crossing the street and you step out too soon, you could be killed. Likewise, if you step into ministry before you have God's green light, it could be detrimental to your life and perhaps the lives of others that you affect.

To everything there is a season. Allow the Holy Spirit to guide you. Don't be in a hurry to be seen or take a front row seat. It is better to allow your gift to make room for you and bring you before great men (Proverbs 18:16).

Just Watch Me

Lastly, I need to tell you that some mentors are silent ones. In other words, you are drawn to the gift of God in them and learn just from watching them operate in their gifting or just observing their lives.

I have such a woman in my life. I call her my silent mentor. Her life speaks volumes to me on being a better wife and a woman of God. If she never says a word from her mouth, her life has spoken all I need. Don't take those silent mentors lightly. They are like directional signs, beacons of light as we walk out our purpose in this life.

Contemplation Time

1. Do I already know what my gifting is? What is it?

_____
_____
_____

2. What do I have a spiritual passion for?

_____
_____
_____

3. What comes naturally to me? (Something that I do without effort.)

_____
_____
_____

4. What type of ministry am I drawn to?

_____
_____
_____

5. Who am I already learning from?

_____
_____
_____

Can I Take Instruction?

"Apply thine heart unto instruction, and thine ears to the words of knowledge."
(Proverbs 23:12; KJV)

This chapter is what I call '*saving the best for last*'. "Can I take instruction" is a difficult question to answer honestly if you answer too quickly. Everyone wants to say, "Yes" to this question because pride demands it. No one wants to admit being unable or unwilling to take instruction.

But this is the time to put pride aside and face the condition of the real inner man. How do you respond as a follower when the person leading is making a decision you don't agree with? Can you carry out instruction without bickering? When behind closed doors do you do it *your way* even if that is contrary to instructions? These questions apply whether it is a spiritual or secular setting.

Taking instruction requires maturity and humility. Humility is required because your pride will often steer you in the opposite direction from where you've been instructed to go. Without some level of humility in operation you will need a helmet for the head banging you will do with leadership.

If you want to save on the aspirin, make a decision that you will walk in humility in your relationships. Humility will help guide you where you need to go.

Think about a toddler being told what to do. The first natural response you get is "NO!"

Stubbornness is a trait we seem to be born with. But the reality is that we learn as we grow that life is more about order and less about getting our own way.

If you are too immature to take instruction, you will come away from any conflict with authority at best feeling it was a waste of time and at worst hurt and offended.

Hebrews 12:11 states: *"Now no chastening for the present seemeth to be joyous, but grievous: nevertheless afterward it yieldeth the peaceable fruit of righteousness unto them which are exercised thereby."*

Love And Correction

A mentoring relationship can be similar to a parent-child relationship. Some days are good and the mentor will say what you want to hear. Other days you wish you could choke them because every word that comes out of their mouth is one you don't want to hear.

No relationship is rosy all the time and a mentoring relationship is no different. In fact I'd be weary of a relationship where everything was always done my way. There's something wrong with that.

However, when the communication you receive from your mentor seems harsh, it is just as necessary to your development as when it's rosy. Let me also mention that mentors have to grow into their role. They may have to learn what the situation warrants.

The mentoring relationship requires both love, which I call honey, and correction, which can be like vinegar. Vinegar is an acid that can be extremely tart when placed in your mouth. It can cause pain like a sour piece of candy.

However if you put these two together it can really be quite palatable. The honey brings a balance of flavor to the vinegar so it goes down easier. You only have to remember that this is for your good so you don't allow the taste of vinegar to overpower the taste of the honey in the relationship.

The Obedience Of The Apostle

Consider if the Apostle Paul had refused to heed the instruction of Jesus on the road to Damascus.

Paul was an active persecutor of the Church and by position alone he could have refused out of arrogance or stubbornness. However, regaining his sight was dependent upon his obedience to the instruction given to him.

Not only that, but sometimes you can't get the directions for the next step if you don't take the first step. Like following a recipe—you must complete each step in order to get to the next one. Can you imagine all the lives that would've been irrevocably affected by Paul's disobedience, including yours?

Paul is the one that teaches that we are more than conquerors and that all things work together for good to them that love God (Romans 8:1, 37).

Paul was one of the most prolific writers ever born. He was responsible for writing most of the New Testament.

If he'd chosen to be disobedient or to selectively obey, we would have missed a wealth of knowledge and encouragement. I dare say some of us would not be living victorious lives today if not for Paul's writings.

But Paul had to go to see Ananias before he ever went on one missionary trip or won one soul to the Lord. Likewise, for all to be done as God ordained, Ananias had to obey God despite his personal feelings about Paul.

God has not changed. He still requires obedience and prefers it to sacrifice. Instruction goes way beyond the moment directly into the future of your children or someone you have yet to meet. We have no idea what is hinged on our willingness to follow instructions.

Moving Beyond The Status Quo

When I graduated from high school I went to nursing school. I was the first one in my family to go to college. Stepping away from what was a pattern in our family brought persecution into my life.

On the flip side, people tend to leave you alone when you follow the status quo and just accept how things have always been. It wasn't always easy, but because I followed a different path, I broke the mold of high school dropouts in my family.

Consequently my children have only known education. It became their norm. By making that one decision, I affected the course of my entire bloodline.

Being able to follow direction will affect you in some ways that you can't even see yet. It is absolutely imperative that you understand the importance of following instruction.

Don't skim over this with a quick "of course I can take instruction". This is too important to the mentoring relationship to skim over or give a response not well thought out. Take a minute to honestly examine yourself by looking at a current relationship with someone in authority.

I selected an authority relationship because the Word tells us to obey them that have the rule over us (Hebrews 13:17). How do you manage your relationships at work or on that committee? Consider this carefully before you answer. Once you can manage your flesh (your pride, ego etc.) you are ready to move on to the next step.

Contemplation Time

1. How well do I take instruction when it's something I don't want to do or from someone I don't like or respect?

_____

_____

2. What do I need to do to separate my feelings from my responsibility?

_____

_____

3. When did I say an unequivocal "YES" to God?

_____

_____

4. What, if anything, have I left undone that He told me to do?

_____

_____

5 What makes me know I am ready to go to the next level of instruction?

_____

_____

6. What will I do when I don't agree and/or when I don't understand?

_____

_____

What Exactly Am I Looking For?

"And ye shall seek me and find me, when ye shall search for me with all your heart."
(Jeremiah 29:13; KJV)

We often foolishly dive headlong into a relationship without even considering what we are searching for. You must have some idea of what it is you are looking for so you will know it when you see it.

You've heard the much quoted saying, "If you fail to plan, you plan to fail". Hence you create a revolving door. You go round and round looking for something that consistently evades you.

In any relationship that you find yourself in, there's always something wrong with *them*. People come and go in your life faster than the seasons change.

For example, if you don't give serious thought to what you want in a church, you will leave more churches than some people ever attend. When you attend a church you may have a preconceived idea of how the people should dress, look or behave. Not that you've thought about your spiritual needs or what you can add to the ministry.

If you enter into the new church with a microscope of criticism, you will eventually find exactly what you need to make you leave with the final verdict being 'it was someone or something that made you leave'.

Whether it's a church or any other relationship, we must be able to stand still and look at ourselves before we move on. I say this because you want to fairly assess the situation and decide what went wrong.

Whatever it is, you don't want to have a repeat performance in the next relationship. This way if the culprit is you, you have the opportunity to deal with yourself and perhaps stay put and see what difference the change makes.

The Outer Package

The divorce rate is as high in the church as in the secular arena. I believe this is because we get married based predominantly on physical attraction, without considering what's inside that beautiful package.

Once you are distracted by outer appearance you are no longer able to objectively look at the person to determine if they are truly compatible with you or your life. Once your emotions enter the equation, subjectivity is not far behind.

So You Want To Be Mentored...

While you previously wrote down what you want in a mate, instead of reviewing your list in prayer, you unconsciously download what you think you see or like about them based on appearance.

If you have done that, you've become the victim of compromise. My husband once told me, after years of marriage, that during the courtship phase you're seeing a performance, not the real behavior you will see from the person on a daily basis.

Anyone that has been married for a while can tell you how superficial looks can be. When the real person shows up after you are married, you forget how good they look and just wonder where in the world did Prince Charming or Cinderella go.

No real relationship can be built or last if it's based on superficial things. It must have substance. It has to be built on something with roots, lest when a storm comes, and it will, the relationship crumbles.

A mentoring relationship is no different. It must also be scrutinized for compatibility and not entered for superficial reasons. It cannot be taken lightly. It has to have a good foundation if it is to withstand the challenges of life.

Therefore it must be prayerfully considered. If you're going to pray, then this might be a good time to fast, as you want to be able to hear God more clearly.

As you pray and fast, be careful not to jot down what you are looking for hurriedly or without thought. Allow time beyond the prayer to meditate on what you think you need.

A Spiritual Or Career Mentor?

When I was a graduate nurse, I learned early on that nurses eat their young. I naively expected to be taught by the older more experienced nurses. As I spent time in my department, I was startled by the number of nurses I encountered that had an attitude of "I got mine, you get yours".

Even though they had the advantage of years of experience and seniority, they were not willing to teach me what they already knew. They preferred that I learn it the hard way. After all, no one showed them the ropes. The problem is that the person in the position to help refuses to do so.

I realized I had two choices. I could perpetuate this attitude and behavior, or I could break the cycle by deciding to take the next young nurse that came along under my wing (once I developed them). It was then that I decided that mentoring though rare was extremely necessary.

Because mentoring is rare, it is important that as you observe and pray over someone you believe could be your mentor; you decide whether you want that individual to function as a spiritual mentor, career mentor or both.

A spiritual mentor is someone who is in relationship with the Lord beyond Sunday and Wednesday (or whatever day Bible study is on).

If you are looking for a spiritual mentor, consider the gifting of the potential mentor. Remember we spoke earlier of trying to put apples with apples. Individuals with a similar gifting to yours will be better able to understand you.

So You Want To Be Mentored...

A spiritual mentor should be someone that loves God, loves God's people and like the Apostle Paul, is *"forgetting those things which are behind, and reaching forth unto those things which are before"* and is pressing toward the mark for the prize of the high calling of God in Christ Jesus (Philippians 3:13-14).

If you are looking for a career mentor, you want to select someone that has been proven over time. It should be someone that you have already been emulating because you esteem them so highly.

But, be careful not to overlook potential mentors, trying to score points with someone that already is out of reach for you at this time.

For example, there are professors from which you could glean. Instead you want to be mentored by the head of the university despite the fact that you are a first year instructor. Don't get me wrong, I want you to aim high, but in a realistic way.

For both the spiritual and career mentors, consider someone that is on a higher level than you, otherwise it's just a peer relationship and those are easy enough to develop. You want someone that can pull you up to another level that you are aspiring to reach.

Consider also the way he/she interacts with others. You will glean this information from your observations. Don't rush in headlong. Just watch. Over time this will allow you to see their response to different situations and circumstances.

However, do not for a moment seek or expect perfection. You will not find that in someone who dwells in a mortal body. If you do, let me know!

Contemplation Time

1. What do I see when I look in the mirror?

_____
_____

2. What are my strengths?

_____
_____

3. What are my weaknesses?

_____
_____

4. Where am I trying to go in life? What are my personal, spiritual and professional goals?

_____
_____

5. What personal needs can I tell the mentor of based on the above information?

_____
_____
_____

6. What strengths do I need my mentor to possess?

_____
_____

How Do I Find a Mentor?

"A word fitly spoken is like apples of gold in pictures of silver."
(Proverbs 25:11; KJV)

Those of you who skipped the previous chapters to come directly to this one have missed the whole point of this book. By doing this, you have already set yourself up for your own failure and the failure of your unsuspecting mentor.

I say this because you have not taken the necessary steps to determine if you are ready to be mentored. You have only decided that you want to be.

For those who have completed the previous chapters, be sure you have not only read the words but completed the tasks. This really is a workbook. Why, because mentoring is a working relationship. Both parties have to participate or it really isn't mentoring.

Have you ever been in a one sided relationship? It is when one person is doing all the giving and the other all the taking. I've been in these. They are exhausting.

I'm not referring to the relationships where you may look up to someone and get advice from them from time to time. I'm talking about the ones where the person will latch on and suck the life's blood out of you with their neediness. You don't want to be needy but as stable as possible if you are seeking a mentor.

Practical application

Beyond the spiritual tools of prayer and fasting, what else can you do to help find a mentor?

Relationships develop differently. Sometimes a relationship will naturally evolve from an existing relationship, like the ones with my moms. Other relationships will have to be cultivated.

I'd like to give you some practical pointers to help you in your search.

A good mentor is both firm and gentle in their approach. Almost anyone can mentor if they are concerned about those coming along behind them.

A good mentor has the ability to see the needs of others and the desire to share what they know. It is very difficult for a selfish person to be a mentor. You must be able to reach out to someone else without expectation of reciprocation.

So You Want To Be Mentored...

There is no special education required. Life is a wonderful teacher and will equip anyone studious enough with the tools they will need to mentor.

1. When you find someone you want to approach and ask to be your mentor, let them know that you would like to speak with them and make an appointment if necessary.

2. Have a prepared plan of what you want and need in a mentoring relationship. Share your plan during the appointment.

3. Ask the potential mentor if they would consider the relationship and be prepared to tell them why you chose them. Also be prepared for "NO" being the answer if he or she feels they can not put in the time and energy that they feel the relationship requires.

4. The frequency of your meetings will depend on what type of mentoring relationship it is and the availability of the mentor. Be prepared to accept what the mentor can give even if it falls short of your complete expectations.

    When I am serving as a baking coach, we may meet once a month. If someone is an organizational training coach, your meetings may be bi-weekly. The frequency of meetings often depends on the need.

5. All mentoring relationships are not created equal. Never judge a present relationship by a past one.

6. The boundaries of the relationship should be established up front in the initial meeting. For example, I do not receive phone calls after 9 p.m. unless it's an emergency.

    Likewise someone who is married may determine that any meetings will take place during the day when the spouse is at work so as not to disturb family time in the evening.

7. How long the relationship lasts depends on what kind of mentor it is. By the time I functioned as an RN for a year, I no longer had the same needs I did as a new graduate.

8. Some mentoring relationships are self-extinguishing. That is to say they run their course without intervention. Don't make the mistake of trying to make all mentoring relationships long-term.

9. Agree on a probationary period, for example: 3-6 months, in order to determine if it's working for both you and the mentor.

10. You can agree at the beginning of the relationship to terminate if it's not working after the probationary period. (If you are not mature enough to

do this, do not enter this type of agreement.) This is why it is important to know yourself.

11. There are some things that are outside of the realm of a mentoring relationship. Don't expect your mentor to be a therapist or counselor, only an advisor.

12. Be prepared to take the advice that you ask for.

13. Refer back to eleven and twelve!

So You Want To Be Mentored...

Contemplation Time

1. What tools do I already employ in looking for a mentor, i.e. do I have a written list of my goals?

_____
_____

2. What steps if any am I taking to look for a mentor?

_____
_____

3. Considering my needs, what gifting does my potential mentor have that line up with what I'm looking for?

_____
_____
_____
_____

4. Am I in the place I need to be in this season of my life? What season am I in?

_____
_____

5. If I am not in the place I need to be, what are some of the things I need to change in order to get there?

_____
_____

Epilogue

In the previous chapters there were a number of questions you were asked to consider before you sought a mentor. Let's revisit these questions:

- **Do I Know Who I Am?**

Do I know who I am or am I looking for someone else to determine this for me? Am I looking for affirmation but confusing it with mentoring because I think a mentor *will* affirm me?

- **Do I Need Emotional Healing?**

Do I need emotional healing, but instead of seeking the healer, I'm looking for a spiritual Band-Aid? Being honest will save you and your mentor a lot of time going around the mountain in the wilderness of your emotional pain.

- **Am I Harboring Unforgiveness?**

Have I chosen to forgive those who have offended or sinned against me, or am I choosing to walk down the self-destructive path of unforgiveness? In order to reap the benefits of mentorship your heart must be free of bitterness lest you be too easily offended to be mentored.

- **Do I Have a Prayer Life?**

On the subject of prayer, ask yourself "Am I expecting my mentor to pray for me?" That's a fair expectation, but will you faithfully pray for your mentor? Being a mentor is a frontline position because you are becoming a covering for someone else. To be successful, someone has to have his/her back in prayer. This is not a trite role. It is completely necessary if you are to get all God has for you out of the mentoring relationship.

- **Do I Know My Gifting?**

Why does the question of gifting arise? If you have no idea of your own gifting it can be like the story I once read where the little duck was going around to all the other animals asking "Are you my mother?" He didn't know if he belonged in a tree or a pond.

- **Can I Take Instruction?**

If you are looking for a mentor, you are looking for a teacher, someone who will lead by wisdom and example. As a parent there were many times I gave instruction to my children that was unwanted as well as unappreciated. Liking the instruction was not a prerequisite to my expectation of obedience. Likewise in a mentoring relationship you may not like what's served, but you need to have already made the decision to clean your plate.

If you have searched your heart concerning the above questions, and found yourself ready to enter into a new season of fruitful mentoring relationships in your life, I applaud you!

I pray that God will bless you beyond what you can imagine, and that as you are mentored by your Naomis, that you will soon look out on the field of your life for the Ruths that are waiting for you!

CONTACT INFORMATION PAGE

Mary Blue: naomi1954@comcast.net

www.ingramcontent.com/pod-product-compliance
Ingram Content Group UK Ltd.
Pitfield, Milton Keynes, MK11 3LW, UK
UKHW041943230426
12048UKWH00008B/111